DISCARDED

ACTION SPORTS
MOTOCROSS

Joe Herran and Ron Thomas

CHELSEA HOUSE
PUBLISHERS
A Haights Cross Communications Company
Philadelphia

Chelsea House Publishers
1974 Sproul Road, Suite 400
Broomall, PA 19008-0914

The Chelsea House world wide web address is www.chelseahouse.com

Library of Congress Cataloging-in-Publication Data

Herran, Joe.
   Motocross / Joe Herran and Ron Thomas.
   p. cm. — (Action sports)

   Includes index.
   Contents: What is motocross? — Motocross gear — Riding safely — Maintaining the bike — Motocross course design — Motocross racing — Skills and techniques — Motocross freestyle — Supercross and Arenacross — In competition: Motocross Grand Prix — Women and motocross — Motocross champions — Then and now — Related action sports.
   ISBN 0-7910-7536-2
   1. Motocross—Juvenile literature. [1. Motocross. 2. Motorcycle racing.] I. Thomas, Ron. II. Title.
   III. Series: Action sports (Chelsea House Publishers).
   GV1060.12.H47 2004
   796.7'56—dc21

                                                                        2003001182

First published in 2003 by
MACMILLAN EDUCATION AUSTRALIA PTY LTD
627 Chapel Street, South Yarra, Australia, 3141

Associated companies and representatives throughout the world.

Edited by Renée Otmar, Otmar Miller Consultancy Pty Ltd, Melbourne
Text and cover design by Karen Young
Illustrations by Nives Porcellato and Andy Craig
Page layout by Raul Diche
Photo research by Legend Images

Printed in China

Acknowledgements

The author and the publisher are grateful to the following for permission to reproduce copyright materials:

Cover photograph: Andrew McFarlane competing in the 2002 Motocross Grand Prix, courtesy of Yamaha.

Australian Picture Library/Corbis, p. 30 (bottom); Australian Picture Library/Sygma, pp. 20, 27 (left); Steven Bonnau, pp. 25, 29; Steve Bruhn, p. 12; Corbis Digital Stock, pp. 4, 5 left, 16–17; Getty Images, pp. 11, 19, 21 (top), 24, 27 (right), 28 (right); Reuters, pp. 5 (top), 5 (bottom right); Phil Smith, pp. 14, 18, 23 (bottom); www.ama-cycle.org, p. 28 (left); Team Suzuki Press Office, p. 23 (top); Yamaha, pp. 7, 8–9, 10, 15, 16 (left), 22, 26, 30 (top); Zeke Vlashi/www.SXdirt.com, p. 21 (bottom).

While every care has been taken to trace and acknowledge copyright, the publisher tenders their apologies for any accidental infringement where copyright has proved untraceable. Where the attempt has been unsuccessful, the publisher welcomes information that would redress the situation.

CONTENTS

INTRODUCTION

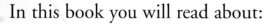

In this book you will read about:

- motocross racing and **freestyle**
- **Supercross** and **Arenacross** events
- the bikes and rider's gear
- safety measures used to keep riders safe

- basic riding skills and techniques
- the top riders in the sport
- the history of the sport from the 1920s.

In the beginning

The word "motocross" comes from the combination of two words, *moto*, the French word for "motorcycle" and *cross*, an abbreviation for "cross-country." The first motocross events were held off-road, on rough tracks over hills and along gullies. The riders seemed to be scrambling all over the track, so the racing became known as **scrambling**. The first races were held in the 1920s in England and became popular during the 1940s and 1950s in Britain and Europe.

Motocross today

Motocross-racing competitions are held at local clubs on specially designed, off-road dirt tracks. National and international competitions are held, as well as a Grand Prix competition developed by the Fédération Internationale de Motocyclisme (FIM).

In the United States, competitors race on circuits built inside large auditoriums and at stadiums. This style of motocross is known as Supercross. Motocross bikes are also used in freestyle-riding events, in which riders perform tricks similar to those performed by BMX freestyle riders.

 **Warning**   This is not a how-to book for aspiring motocross riders. It is intended as an introduction to the exciting world of motocross, and a look at where the sport has come from and where it is heading.

WHAT IS MOTOCROSS?

There are three types of motocross riding: motocross track racing—including Motocross Grand Prix—Supercross and motocross freestyle.

Motocross track racing

Motocross track races are fast, close and exciting events, held on off-road tracks about 1.2 miles (2 kilometers) long. The tracks contain left and right bends, bumps known as **whoops**, jumps, hills and gullies. These test both the riders' skills and their machines.

↗ Motocross riders roar away from the starting gate at the 2002 Bulgarian Motocross Grand Prix.

Supercross

Supercross is motocross racing on specially built tracks in indoor and outdoor stadiums. Spectators watch as riders race around steeply banked corners and fly over **tabletop** jumps. Supercross events can be held at night under the stadium lights.

Motocross freestyle

Motocross freestyle riders perform tricks on their bikes. They jump over obstacles and off ramps, performing as many tricks as possible.

↙ A motocross freestyle rider performs a trick high in the air.

↗ Spectators at Supercross events watch spectacular motorcycle racing at the first-ever Supercross event held in Cambodia, in 2002.

MOTOCROSS GEAR

The motocross bike

Bikes used for motocross are specially made to be ridden at high speed on rough tracks. They are built for strength and fast acceleration. They provide the power needed to climb hills and cross muddy surfaces.

Two-stroke engine

The engine is the mechanism that makes the bike run. Fuel is mixed with air as it is sucked into the motor, where it is burned to create the energy that drives the **pistons**. The rider controls the engine power with the throttle. The engine is mounted high off the ground to be well clear of the ground when the rider performs jumps. An aluminum glide plate is fitted to protect the bottom of the engine.

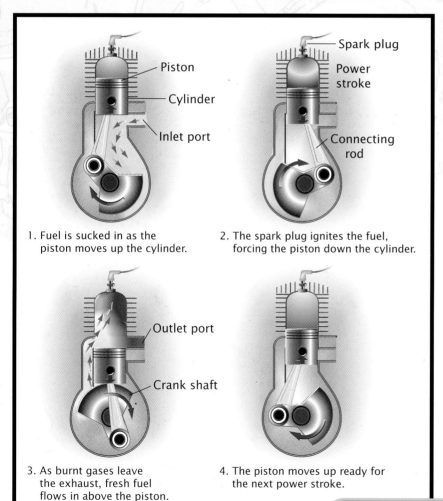

1. Fuel is sucked in as the piston moves up the cylinder.

2. The spark plug ignites the fuel, forcing the piston down the cylinder.

3. As burnt gases leave the exhaust, fresh fuel flows in above the piston.

4. The piston moves up ready for the next power stroke.

TWO-STROKE ENGINE

Wheels and tires

Wheels are spoked. Spokes keep the wheel rims round and absorb the shock of bumps. Tires have deep-cut, chunky treads to grip all kinds of racetrack surfaces.

Chain and sprockets

The chain transfers power from the engine to drive the back wheel. The sprockets link the rim of the wheel to the chain.

Brakes

Disc brakes are used for fast braking. The rider controls the front-wheel brake with a right-hand lever. The rear-wheel brake is controlled with the right foot.

Front forks and shock absorbers

Shock absorbers are fitted inside the front **forks** to cushion the rider from the bumpy track and when landing after a jump. Motocross bikes also have rear shock absorbers.

ACTION FACT

Quiet and less smoky **two-stroke engines** with fuel-injection systems are being designed and built for motocross. This will make the bikes more environmentally friendly.

Throttle   Footpeg   Chain   Wheel

Front fork   Engine   Sprockets   Tire

The motocross rider's gear

Helmet

The helmet protects the head in a fall. It is designed to reduce the effect of wind and noise on the rider.

Goggles

The goggles must be tough enough to withstand being hit by dirt and stones that are thrown up from the track. Goggles protect the rider's eyes from the wind.

Race shirt

Race shirts are mostly cotton or polyester. Polyester is cooler than cotton. It does not stretch as quickly and is easier to screen print with team colors and symbols.

Body armor

Body armor consists of a chest protector, shoulder pads and a kidney belt. The chest protector is worn under the shirt to shield the rider from things thrown up from the track by other bikes. The kidney belt is worn around the waist on top of the shirt but under the pants to support the rider's back.

Race pants

The pants are usually made of nylon, a tough synthetic material that is comfortable to wear.

Gloves

Gloves are designed to allow the rider's hands and wrists to move freely. There are **carbon-fiber** inserts on the knuckles and **Kevlar** padding for protection.

Motocross boots

Boots should be comfortable and have a strong buckle system. A carbon fiber inner shell and a leather outer layer reinforce the ankles and toes for extra protection.

Pads, braces and guards

Knee pads and knee braces protect the knees from injury when falling. Elbow guards, worn under the race shirt, protect the elbows and upper arms.

Body armor

Helmet

Race shirt

Elbow guards

Goggles

Race pants

Gloves

Motocross boots

Knee pads

RIDING
SAFELY

Motocross riders should follow these basic rules to keep themselves and others safe and injury-free:

- check that the helmet is clean and undamaged
- check that goggles are cleaned after every race and, when not in use, stored where they will not get scratched
- check that gloves, body armor and other protective clothes are clean and in good condition
- learn the basic skills of speed control, turning, braking, and stopping on flat ground

- know how to ride within their personal limits; that is, to know when to slow down if losing control of the bike
- look ahead for obstacles and signs of danger
- obey the rules made to protect riders and spectators
- take a practice run on a new course or walk the course before a race to learn what it is like
- never ride alone when practicing in case of an accident
- drink plenty of water; **dehydration** can cause a rider to suffer muscle cramps and loss of concentration.

Before a race, a rider should take a practice-run to learn the course.

Getting ready to ride

Motocross racing is a physically demanding sport. Almost every muscle in a rider's body is used while racing, so the rider must be fit and strong. To maintain their fitness and build strength, riders run, swim, cycle or play sports such as football. Being fit helps a rider to perform well and enjoy the sport. A healthy diet is important for fitness, too.

Warming up

Gentle stretching, jogging or jumping will warm up and loosen a rider's muscles before a race. Warm, loose muscles work better and are less likely to cramp. Doing some simple exercises before riding may help the rider avoid injuries such as torn ligaments and sprains.

Training professional riders

Professional motocross riders have trainers who help them to keep fit and ready to compete. Trainers plan a program of exercises to make the rider's muscles strong. They also plan food programs to make sure that the riders eat a healthy and balanced diet.

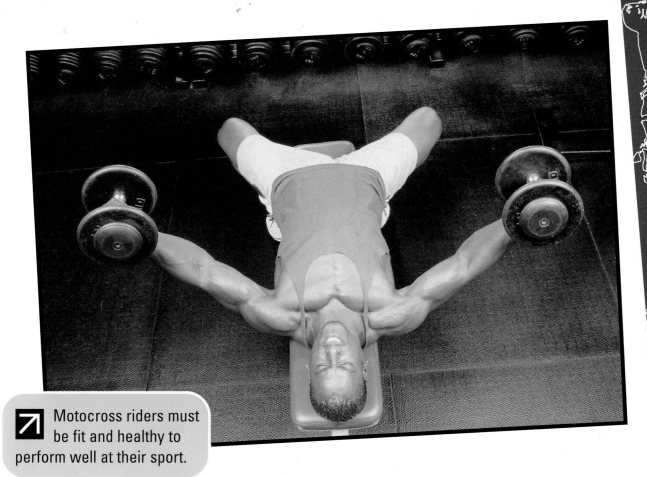

↗ Motocross riders must be fit and healthy to perform well at their sport.

MAINTAINING THE
BIKE

Motorcycles can be dangerous machines to ride. Therefore, it is important that the rider regularly checks the bike to make sure it is working well.

Regular checks on the bike include:

- inspecting tires for damage
- checking tire pressure
- checking that the wheel spokes are not bent or loose
- checking that the brakes are working properly
- checking that the chain is well lubricated with oil
- checking that oil and fuel are at proper levels
- making sure that there are no loose or missing screws or bolts anywhere on the bike.

↗ Regular mechanical checks are essential for safe riding.

MOTOCROSS COURSE DESIGN

There are hundreds of motocross courses in countries around the world. Each has its own special design, with turns, hills and jumps. The FIM has set out some specifications for the design and construction of motocross-racing courses.

- The course has to be between 0.9 and 1.8 miles (1.5 and 3 kilometers) in length, and not less than 16.4 feet (5 meters) wide at the narrowest point.
- Multiple jumps (double or triple jumps) are forbidden.
- The distance between jumps must be a minimum of 98 feet (30 meters) from the top of a jump to the bottom of the next jump.
- The design of the track should allow bikes to travel at a maximum speed of 34 miles (55 kilometers) per hour.
- The width of the track at the start line must allow for at least 30 bikes.
- Straw bales and other effective shock-absorbent material must be set up as safety barriers to protect the riders from all obstacles.
- The track must be free of big stones, and any that come to the surface during the race must be removed.

Safety barriers

Jump

Finish

Jump

Start

Jump

A MOTOCROSS COURSE MAP

MOTOCROSS RACING

Races for amateur riders, known as motos, can last 15 to 25 minutes. Professional riders may race for up to 45 minutes.

The course

Most courses are between 0.9 and 1.8 miles (1.5 and 3 kilometers) long. Each course is made of dirt, with gullies, hills and a number of banked bends called **berms**. There are also bumpy sections of the track called whoops. The tabletop is a jump with a flat top and a ramp at the end.

The start

At the start of the race, the riders line up with their bikes on a starting pad behind the starting gate. Hand brakes are held on to keep the bikes from rolling into the gate. In motocross, most gates fall backwards, so they trap the front wheel of any bike whose rider tries to get an early start. When the gate falls, the riders, leaning forward, accelerate to full power and take off, engines roaring.

Getting the best start in a race is known as **holeshot**.

14

SKILLS AND TECHNIQUES

Riding: the correct body position

The correct body position for the motocross rider is with the rider's weight in the center of the motorcycle. The head is above the handlebars, looking ahead for obstacles. The feet on the **footpegs** and bent knees carry most of the rider's weight. The elbows are held high and away from the body. The rider's fingers are held ready on the handlebar control levers.

Braking

Brakes are used to reduce speed and to help the rider hold position and balance during a turn. The front brake is operated from the handlebars, while the rear brake is controlled with a foot pedal. A rider is usually standing when using the brakes, with the weight of the body toward the back of the bike for greater control. Riders apply the brakes smoothly to avoid the bike spinning or sliding.

Riders who learn the correct body position are able to ride longer because they stay relaxed and use less energy.

Cornering

A rider is usually in a sitting position when turning, with his weight to the front of the bike to help the front wheels keep a grip of the track. The rider approaches the corner fast and applies the brakes just before beginning the turn. The brake is off for the turn and, if necessary, the rider drags a foot in the dirt for balance. When coming out of the turn, the rider speeds up again.

Jumping

During a jump, the rider stands up with knees bent, arms up and elbows bent. The rider controls the angle of the bike in the air by shifting their weight backward or forward. On landing, the rear wheel usually touches the ground first. If a rider falls during a jump, they may get up and continue in the race, as long as the motorcycle has not been damaged.

A rider stands up with knees bent, arms up and elbows bent during a jump.

16

Passing another rider

Riders may pass each other anywhere on the track. The best and safest place for one rider to pass another is on the **straight**. The rider wishing to pass must accelerate to speed by the other rider. However, most passing is done at corners. The rider wanting to pass follows a different line to the rider in front, and tries to pass on the inside. Another passing technique is for the rider wanting to pass to go out wide at the corner, speed around the corner and head off the rider in front. Riders often prepare for passing during a race by walking the course before race time, looking for good places to pass.

 Most riders try to pass one another at corners.

MOTOCROSS FREESTYLE

Freestyle competition events take place on a dirt track that includes jumps, **spines**, obstacles and ramp-to-ramp **transitions**.

Motocross freestyle bikes

Some parts of motocross bikes used in freestyle are altered slightly so that riders can use them when performing tricks.

- The handlebars are tapered.
- The seat is shoved down so the rider can stand on it.
- The side number plates have holes in them for the rider's feet.
- The footpegs are larger than normal to give the rider a good footing.

Freestyle bikes are altered to make it easier for riders to perform tricks.

Some freestyle tricks

Many tricks used in freestyle motocross are similar to those performed by BMX freestyle riders.

CLIFFHANGER

While in the air, the rider leaves the bike, raises the hands above the head, holding onto the handlebars with the feet. This is considered a very difficult trick!

CAN CAN

The rider takes one foot off the footpeg and raises the leg up and over the seat so that both legs are on the same side of the bike.

Freestyle competition

The first motocross freestyle competitions were held in 1996. Since 1999, motocross freestyle has become a regular event in both the X Games and the Gravity Games. An international organization, the International Freestyle Motocross Association (IFMA) has been formed to organize an annual World Championship of freestyle motocross. Riders practice during the day for a night competition. Riders compete in heats to qualify for the main event. The finalists compete in a 2-minute final run, performing as many tricks as they can.

Judges award points for:

- style (how good the rider looks while performing)
- the degree of difficulty of each trick
- continuity (how well the tricks link from one to another)
- originality (how different the rider's performance is from others).

ACTION FACT

Step Up is a type of freestyle motocross event in which riders jump their bikes over a high-jump bar. The highest jump to date was performed by American Tommy Clowers in 2000. He drove up a take-off ramp and jumped his bike 35 feet (10.67 meters) over the bar.

Riders perform daring tricks to score points from the judges.

SUPERCROSS AND ARENACROSS

Supercross is motocross racing over specially built tracks in indoor and outdoor stadiums. In preparation for the events, huge earth-moving machines move the dirt used to make the jumps, whoops and berms. Spectators watch from stadium seats as the riders race around the steeply banked corners and fly over tabletop jumps.

Arenacross is motocross racing held on a specially built track in an indoor arena. Events include 20-lap races for professional riders, amateur races, the "Dash for Cash," which is a four-lap, no-rules race, and an extreme jump-off contest in which riders perform aerial acrobatic stunts 65 feet (20 meters) in the air. Arenacross events are staged in the United States, Canada and Europe, where riders compete for millions of dollars in prize money.

ACTION FACT

The first indoor motocross events, which would later become Supercross, were held in the 1960s.

Supercross events can be held at night under the stadium lights.

This Arenacross competition is in Bridgeport, Conneticut.

IN COMPETITION: MOTOCROSS
GRAND PRIX

Grand Prix Motocross racing is organized and run by the FIM. The FIM has established a sporting code of rules and regulations for motocross racing, as well as technical rules to ensure that all racing bikes are safe. Grand Prix motocross bikes come in three classifications: 125 **cc**, 250 cc and 500 cc. All three classifications have their final race on the day of the Grand Prix. For the 2002 Motocross Grand Prix season, races were held in 13 countries.

Grand Prix motocross racing events are held on specially built circuits which, according to FIM rules, must not be too bumpy and must be built in such a way to keep speeds down to below 34 miles (55 kilometers) per hour. There must be barriers to protect spectators from race accidents. Straw bales and other shock-absorbing materials are used to protect the riders from danger. Protective coverings are placed around trees, poles and other obstacles on the course.

Australian **MX** rider Andrew McFarlane competed in the 2002 Grand Prix motocross circuit.

The World Champion rider

Grand Prix points are awarded to the winning rider, to other place-getters and to their teams. The winner of a Grand Prix is awarded 25 points, second place 20 points, third place 16 points and the rider in fourth place gets 13 points. At the end of the season, the rider with the most points is the World Champion.

Officials

Officials on the Grand Prix circuit are responsible for ensuring that the race is safe for spectators and riders. All motorcycles are checked carefully before the start of the race. At any time during the race an official may ask a rider to leave the track if the official believes that a motorcycle is unsafe.

↖ The riders who finish the race in first, second and third positions attend a prize-giving ceremony on the podium immediately after the race.

Official signals

Signals are given by officials to the riders by means of flags. For example, a red flag means that all riders must stop, and a yellow flag held still means that there is danger and riders must go slowly.

↗ A black-and-white checkered flag signals the end of the race.

23

WOMEN AND MOTOCROSS

In England in the 1920s and 1930s, women motorcyclists competed against men in many motorcycle events. Two of the best women riders at this time were Fay Taylour from Ireland and Eva Askquith from England. Taylour was such a good rider that in 1929 she was invited to tour Australia, where she rode in Perth and Brisbane.

Around this time, in England there was a push to ban women from motocross competition. In 1930, after rider Vera Hole fell from her bike and broke her collarbone, a ban on women competitors came into effect. Although women were still allowed to compete in motorcycle events in Europe, the United States and Australia, few women did so.

In the United States in the 1970s, an association of women motorcyclists was formed. The association was called PowderPuffs Unlimited Riders and Racers (PURR), and it organized a number of motorcycling events for women. In 1975, ten top women riders competed in the Women's Invitational Trophy Dash, held at the Los Angeles Coliseum before 80,000 fans.

In the 1990s, the Women's Motocross League was formed. It organized a series of races in the United States. In 2001, the League organized a season of nine racing events running from May through to September and open to female MX (motocross) riders from around the world.

In New Zealand, Australia, Sweden, Italy and England, women's motocross organizations stage regular competitions.

Fay Taylour at the Crystal Palace Speedway in London, in 1934.

Motocross racing is a popular sport run on specially designed, off-road dirt tracks. There are local, national and international competitions, as well as a Grand Prix competition. Some of the top riders of motocross come from Europe, including Italy and Belgium. There is also a United States motocross circuit called the Supercross for champion riders from the United States and Canada. Freestyle motocross has developed mostly in the United States. Top riders compete in freestyle motocross as part of the Gravity Games and both the Summer and Winter X Games.

MOTOCROSS
CHAMPIONS

↗ Tania Satchwell

• Born February 5, 1980 in Napier, New Zealand

Career highlights

• Women's Motocross League (WML) Champion in 2001

• Has won New Zealand Women's National Championship seven times

↗ Stefy Bau

• Born February 17, 1978 in Milan, Italy

Career highlights

• Runner-up WML Champion in 2001

• WML International Cup Pro 125 cc and 250 cc; WML National Pro Champion in 1999

• Has won Italian Women's National Championship seven times

↗ Stefan Everts

- Born November 25, 1972, Belgium
- Began racing motocross in 1982, riding an 80 cc motorbike
- His father, Harry, is a former motocross world champion
- Has won a World Championship in each division of motocross competition

Career highlights

- Came third in 125 cc World Championship in 1990
- 125 cc World Champion in 1991
- Came second in 250 cc World Championship in 1994
- 250 cc World Champion, member of the Belgian team that won the Motocross des Nations in 1995
- 250 cc World Champion in 1996 and 1997
- 500 cc World Champion in 2001
- Won the Netherlands 500 cc MX Grand Prix in 2002

↗ Marnicq Bervoets

- Born June 21, 1969, Belgium
- Has been in the top five of the FIM World Championships for the past 9 years

Career highlights

- Belgian Champion 250 cc in 1994, 1996 and 1999
- Came second in the 250 cc World Championships in 1995, 1996 and 1997
- Member of the Belgian team that won the Motocross des Nations in 1997
- Came second in the 500 cc World Championships in 2000
- Came third in the 500 cc World Championships in 2001

FREESTYLE AND SUPERCROSS CHAMPIONS

↗ Travis Pastrana

- Born October 8, 1983, Annapolis, Maryland
- Competes in Supercross 125 cc racing and in Freestyle motocross

Career highlights

- Winner of Freestyle competitions at the X Games and the Gravity Games in 1999
- Winner of seven 125 cc Supercross races in 2000
- Winner of Freestyle competition X Games, came eighth in Freestyle Step Up in 2000
- Winner of eight 125 cc Supercross races in 2001
- Winner of Freestyle competition at the X Games and the Gravity Games, came second in Freestyle Step Up in 2001

↗ Jeremy McGrath

- Born November 19, 1971, San Francisco, California
- Began motorcycle racing at age 14 and became a professional rider in 1989
- Has won more races than any other rider
- Probably the most famous Supercross racer in the world

Career highlights

- Won his first 250 cc Supercross Championship in 1993
- Won 250 cc Supercross Championship, winning 9 of 15 races, in 1994
- Won 250 cc Supercross Championship in 1995 and 1996
- American Motorcyclist Association (AMA) Pro Athlete of the Year in 1996
- Won 250 cc Supercross Championship in 1998, 1999 and 2000
- Finished second in the 250 cc Supercross Championship in 2001

THEN AND NOW

1885	1892	1896	1904	1907	1924	1930s
Gottlieb Daimler built the first motorcycle. The bike had smaller outrigger wheels on each side and was made of wood.	The first two-wheeled motorbike, the Millet, was built. It had an engine in the hub of its rear wheel.	The first major motorbike race was held in France, on roads between the cities of Paris and Nantes, over a distance of 94.5 miles (152 kilometers). Some competitors rode motor tricycles!	The first international race, the Coupe International, a 170-mile (273-kilometer) event, was held in France. French rider Demester won at an average speed of 45 miles (72.5 kilometers) per hour. The Fédération Internationale des Clubs Motorcyclists was formed to regulate motorcycle racing throughout Europe.	The first motorcycle race circuit was built in Britain. The circuit was 2.8 miles (4.5 kilometers) in length and was egg-shaped.	The first scramble was held in Britain. Scrambling later became known as motocross racing.	Women were banned from motorcycle racing in England.

1885

1924

1947	1970s	1974	1996	1998	1999	2001
The first International Motocross des Nations were held between teams of five riders from Great Britain, France, Belgium and Holland.	Powder Puff Derby motorcycle races for women began in the United States.	The first motocross-racing circuits were started in the United States.	The Women's Motocross League was formed to support female motocross riders around the world.	The first freestyle motocross events were held. The International Freestyle Motocross Association (IFMA) was formed to organize annual World Championship competitions.	Jeremy McGrath won his 77th Supercross race, becoming the all-time winner of Supercross races.	Women's motocross events were organized in the United States, Sweden, United Kingdom and Australia.

Heidi Henry, 23, from Visalia, California, was the only woman freestyle motocross rider in the world in 2001. |

2001

RELATED ACTION
SPORTS

Enduro

Enduro is long-distance, cross-country racing along narrow bush trails and on fast, open tracks. Riders must get past obstacles and ride through water and mud as quickly as they can. Riders race against the clock to record the fastest time.

↗ World champion rider Max Biaggi has won more than 23 Grand Prix motorcycle races.

Motorcycle Grand Prix racing

Grand Prix motorcycle racing events are held on specially built circuits. Bikes built using the most advanced technology come in three classifications: 125 cc, 250 cc and 500 cc. This spectacular sport is enjoyed by millions of spectators worldwide.

Trials riding

Trials riding is motorcycle riding using a specially designed bike. Riders must ride over obstacles such as rocks, tree trunks and deeply rutted tracks without taking their feet off the footpegs. In competition, a rider is penalized if the feet or hands touch the ground.

↘ Trials riding tests the skill and balance of a rider.

GLOSSARY

Arenacross motocross racing held on specially built tracks in indoor arenas

berms built-up corners of the track

cc cubic capacity, relating to the size of the engine

carbon fiber a rigid but light substance used to pad gloves

dehydration the loss of water or moisture from the body

footpegs footrests on the bottom portion of the bike frame

forks the parts of the bike that secure the front wheel to the handlebars and absorb bumps as the bike crosses rough ground

freestyle a contest in which riders are given a set time to perform a variety of jumps and aerial tricks for a judged score

holeshot a motocross rider who gets the best start and grabs the lead

Kevlar a material that is extremely strong and heat-resistant

MX an abbreviation for motocross

pistons cylinders which move backward and forward in an engine tube to give it power

scrambling a 1920s term for motocross racing

spines two launch ramps sitting back-to-back with a small deck between them

straight the part of a motor-racing track without a bend or curve

Supercross the highest competitive level of motocross racing in the United States; also any race held in an arena or stadium on built obstacles

tabletop a jump with a flat top and a landing ramp at the end

transitions parts of the ramp that curve upwards

two-stroke engines having an engine cycle in which one piston stroke out of every two is a power stroke

whoops a bumpy section of the motocross track

INDEX